MYSTERIES
OF THE ANCIENT WORLD

THE HOLY SHROUD

TRISTAN GRAY HULSE

WEIDENFELD & NICO
LONDON

On the night of 28 May 1898 Secondo Pia clambered up on to a specially constructed platform in front of the high altar of the cathedral in Turin. He had been asked to photograph a length of ancient closely woven linen exhibited in an elaborate frame above the altar. Using his cumbersome camera and relying on the usually less-than-reliable electric lights of the period, which had already defeated his attempts to photograph the cloth on 25 May, Pia slowly exposed two glass plates. Then he took the plates back to his studio to develop them.

Giulio Clovio (1498–1578), **The Holy Shroud of Turin.**

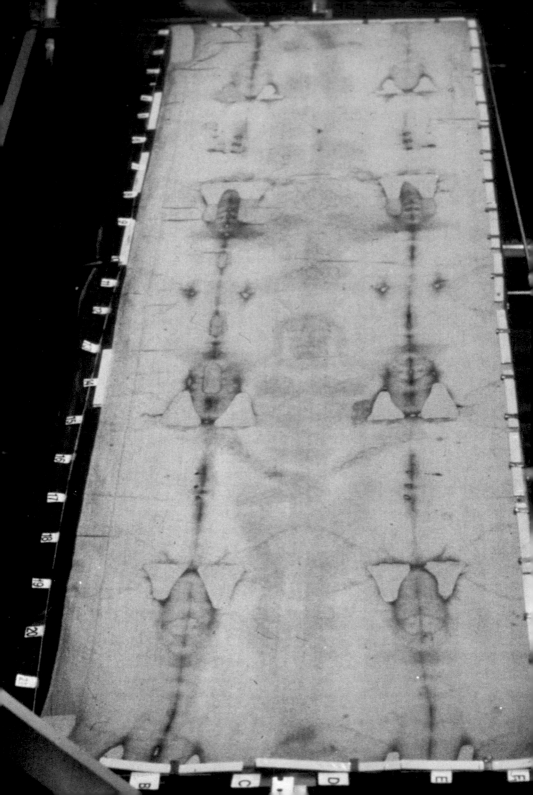

The Shroud Rediscovered

For centuries, this ancient linen cloth, measuring approximately 4.5 x 1.1 m, has been venerated as the actual burial shroud of Jesus Christ. The cloth shows, in a faint and shadowy way, the front and rear images of a dead man. These images are sepia-coloured, with reddish marks suggesting blood-stains at the wrists, feet and side of the dead man – the whole seemingly recording the impressions made when the body of a man executed in the most barbarous of manners was laid upon one half of the cloth, and the other half was folded over him. The supposed blood-stains basically conform to the accounts of the crucifixion of Jesus given in the Gospels.

It was this vague image which Signor Pia expected to see when he developed his plates. What he in fact saw created an immediate sensation and has generated controversy ever since, for Pia's negatives revealed, not the shadowy image on the Shroud itself, but a fully rounded and extraordinarily detailed portrait of the Man on the Shroud. Pia believed – and since then millions have shared his conviction – that he was gazing, for the first time in history, upon the actual face of Jesus.

The news, and the new images, rapidly spread across the world, and battle-lines were quickly formed, for and against the integrity of the Shroud as a real relic of Christ and the genuineness or otherwise of its astounding image. In France in 1902 Professor Yves Delage, himself an agnostic, scandalized the august French Academy by telling them that the Shroud was the true burial-cloth of Jesus. At the same time the biologist Paul Vignon conducted researches which appeared to show that the images on the Shroud conformed

The image of Jesus Christ as seen on the Shroud of Turin.

The face of Jesus as first seen by Secondo Pia in 1898 (negative and positive images).

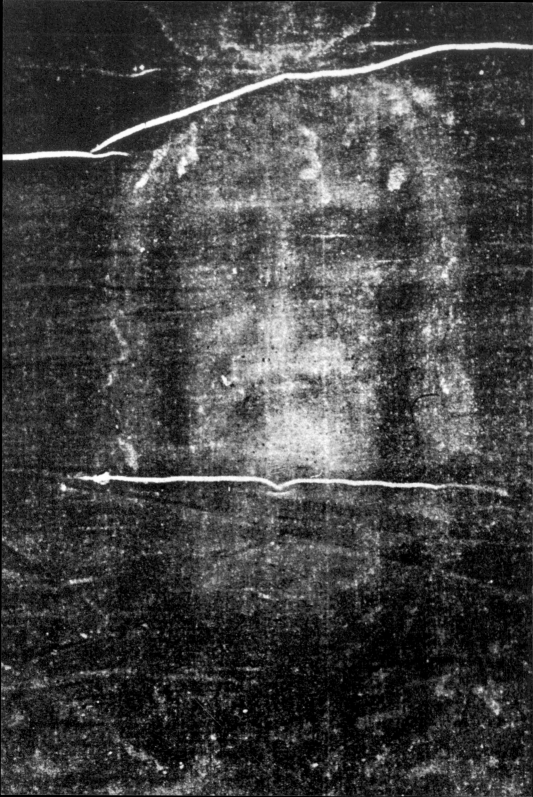

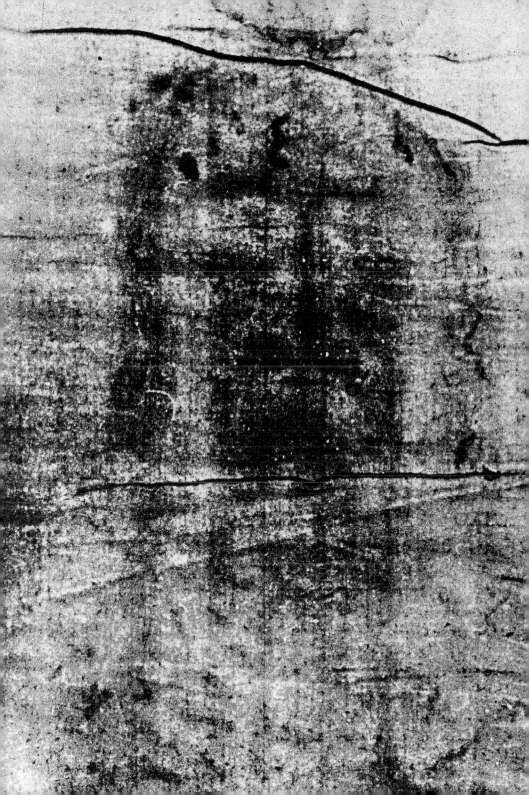

exactly to the procedures of an actual crucifixion, and his iconographic studies demonstrated that the newly revealed face of Jesus was significantly similar to the images of Jesus accepted as such by the Church since earliest times. Vignon's subsequent books have been greatly influential. Also at this period, the Frenchman Ulysse Chevalier and the English Jesuit Herbert Thurston, both of them Catholic priests who based their work on medieval documentation of the Shroud, roundly condemned it as a forgery, the work of some medieval artist. To this day, scientific and historic interest in the Shroud is similarly polarized.

Since 1898, thousands of photographs have been taken of the Holy Shroud. Each one has clearly revealed, in photographic negative, an image of startling clarity and sophistication – an image, as so many have readily believed, that could not have been deliberately fabricated today, let alone by a medieval forger. Groups of experts assembled to try to decipher the riddle of the

The image of Christ 'Not-Made-By-Hands' (12th-century icon, School of Vladimir-Suzdal).

9

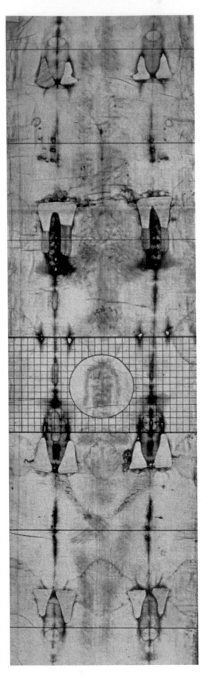

Modern photo-graph of the Shroud marked in illustration of Ian Wilson's Shroud/Mandylion theory.

The shrine of the Holy Shroud in Turin Cathedral.

Shroud, but, following the tradition of centuries, the Holy Shroud was exposed to view only once or twice each hundred years, thus permitting few chances for proper investigation. An initial scientific examination was organized by the archbishop of Turin in 1969, and in 1973 the Swiss criminologist Max Frei took pollen samples from the surface of the cloth. From these, he was able to argue that the Shroud had indeed been in all the places it was known or might validly be suggested to have been in the years since the crucifixion and burial of Jesus. This seemed impressive, but in 1977 a conference of US scientists in Albuquerque, New Mexico, became the prelude to what was to be a seemingly much more conclusive series of tests.

In 1978 the Holy Shroud was removed from its shrine in the Royal Chapel of Turin Cathedral, and exhibited for veneration. Over six weeks,

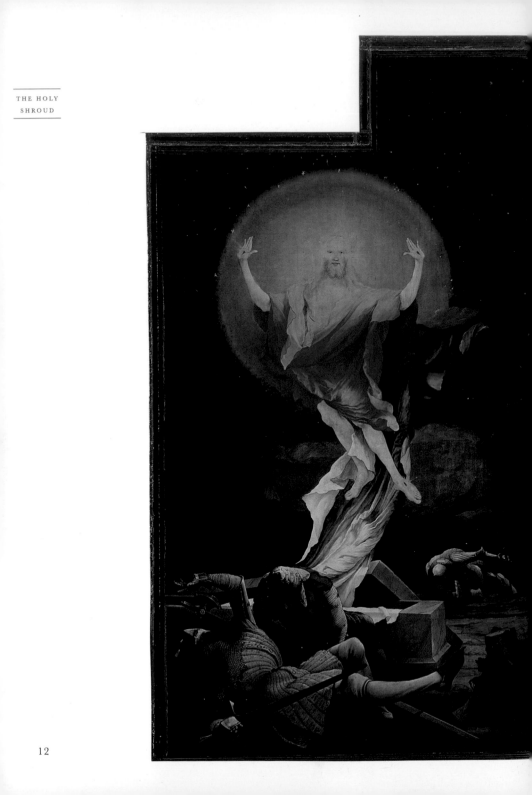

*The glory of the Resurrection,
as depicted by
Matthias Grünewald (1477–1528).*

13

more than three million people came to see it. Afterwards, between 8 and 12 October, it was the object of intensive study by the US-based Shroud of Turin Research Project (STURP), when some 25 scientists subjected it to an extraordinary variety of tests. The team's photographer, Vernon Miller, took the most detailed and beautiful series of photographs available to date. The findings were astounding. The sepia body-image was found to be entirely on the surface of the fabric, rather than absorbed into it; which meant that the image was formed in some way other than by simple contact with the bloody, sweat-soaked body of Jesus, as had previously been supposed. At the same time, the substance of the reddish stains was revealed as consonant with the chemical constituents of real blood.

To many, it seemed that the Shroud had finally been vindicated. Speculation turned to the actual nature of the image, and its formation. Some scientists were even prepared to suggest that the image had been somehow 'burned' on to the cloth, by a burst of radiation energy released during Christ's resurrection. There seemed little left but admiration and awe in the presence of so numinous an object.

What is the Shroud?

The impressive and beautiful face on the Shroud has always been an important factor in persuading people that the Man on the Shroud is indeed Jesus. There are numbers of ancient traditions which tell that Jesus left his facial image imprinted on cloth, images 'not-made-by-hands', which were treasured and venerated and copied, thus becoming the prototypes of the standard images of Christ familiar from centuries of Christian art. That such traditional images and their derivatives conform to the Shroud face had been noted by Vignon, and his iconographic conclusions were substantially augmented in 1978, when

Eighteenth-century devotional print of the icon preserved in San Bartolomeo, Genoa, once believed to be the Mandylion.

Effigies Christi Domini.

Ex ipsomet Divino Exemplari AD ABGARUM *missa Genuæ in Ecclesia* Sti Bartolomæi
Clericorum Reg. Sti Pauli *Summa Veneratione asservato*

Accuratissime Expressa.

Dr Alan Whanger devised a technique for overlaying the Shroud image with images from ancient icons of Jesus. In many instances, he was able to show up to 170 points of similarity between the images; thereby demonstrating to his satisfaction that the face was actually the original from which the iconic type was derived. This is an important point, given the known history of the Shroud.

At one time there were numbers of *acheiropoietos,* or 'not-made-by-hands', images of Christ's face to be found throughout Christendom, such as the Mandylion of Edessa and the Veil of Veronica, and these are known from a multitude of copies. Some of them, it is claimed, survive even today, and research shows that this whole group of images corresponds in striking detail to the face on the Shroud. It is surprising, then, to learn that the majority of these alternative portraits of Christ, all of which can be shown to be the works of human artists, have a demonstrable history far older than that of the Shroud. For the Turin Shroud is first recorded in the 14th century.

The Shroud in History

In 1353 the knight Geoffrey de Charny founded a collegiate church at Lirey, in France. In 1356 he was killed fighting the English at the battle of Poitiers, and the Shroud is heard of for the first time in the following year, when his widow Jeanne exhibited it to pilgrims. Where it came from, or how it came into the keeping of the de Charnys, is nowhere so much as hinted at. Modern researchers have tried to provide a provenance for it. The most coherent attempt is that of Ian Wilson, the British author of a number of books on the Shroud, who suggested that it should be identified with the Edessa Mandylion,

St Veronica, between Saints Peter and Paul, displays her veil marked with the image of Christ (Albrecht Dürer, 1511).

traceable to the 6th century, which was transferred to the imperial relic hoard in Constantinople in 944. There a cloth which appears to have looked rather

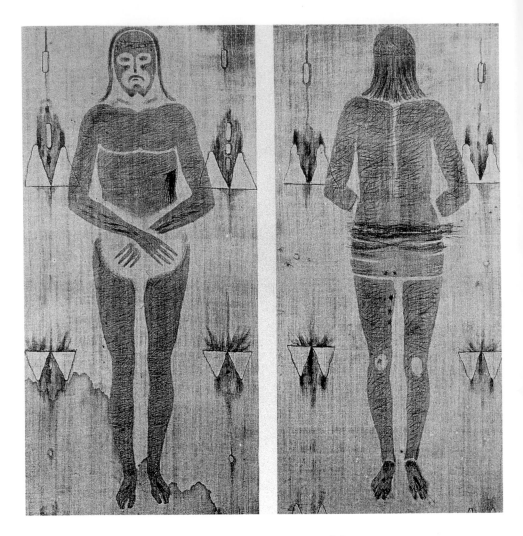

Sixteenth-century copy of the Holy Shroud preserved in Nôtre-Dame de Chambéry (sepia watercolour on cloth).

like the Shroud, and which was described as 'the sydoine in which our Lord had been wrapped', was seen by the Frenchman Robert de Clari in 1203. Wilson postulated that the Mandylion/sydoine/Shroud was looted from Constantinople in 1204, and eventually brought to France by the Templars, one of whom, Geoffrey de Charny, may have been related to the Lirey de Charnys. The story is ingenious rather than convincing, but that the relic came from Constantinople is plausible enough.

Its subsequent history is well documented. In 1418 the Lirey canons placed the Shroud for safe-keeping with Jeanne and Geoffrey's granddaughter Margaret, who in 1453 gave it to Duke Louis of Savoy. The House of Savoy eventually placed the cloth in the so-called Sainte-Chapelle, their family chapel in Chambéry, which was restored and beautified as a fitting shrine for the Shroud.

Today, the most obvious thing seen on the Shroud is not the pale image, but two rows of patches, stains and scorches, which run the entire length of the cloth on either side of the figure. These result from an accident that almost destroyed the mysterious secret of the Shroud centuries before it was revealed. On 4 December 1532 fire broke out in the Sainte-Chapelle, and by the time the Shroud was rescued its silver reliquary had begun to melt. Molten drops of metal dripped along one edge of the folded cloth, burning right through the entire relic. Two years later nuns patched the linen and the expositions began again.

The Shroud was the most prized possession of the House of Savoy, and when they moved their capital to Turin, it was inevitable that it should move with them, in 1578. It remained in the palace chapel, the focus of ever-increasing devotion, until 1694, when it was transferred to a sumptuous purpose-built Baroque chapel in the cathedral. Here it has remained ever since. The Shroud remained the property of the Savoy royal family until 1983, when ex-King Umberto II bequeathed it to the pope on his deathbed.

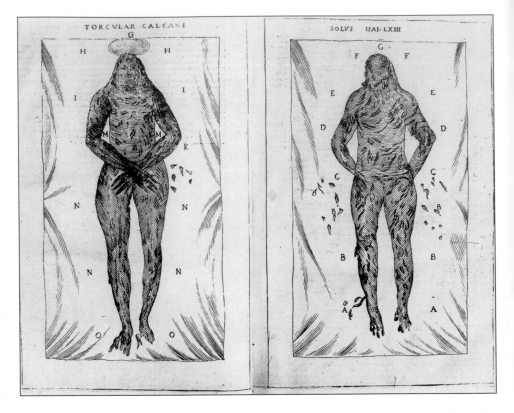

*A*rtist's impression illustrating
an early book on the Shroud
(F. D. Malloni, **Stigmata Sacrae
Sindoni Impressa,** *1606).*

*S*eventeenth-century Spanish
painting of Christ cradled in
a blood-stained shroud: José de
Ribera (1591–1652), **The Trinity.**

Though increasingly the Shroud came to be seen as evidently self-vindicat-
ing, the Church itself has never pronounced on it, preferring to see it as a mag-
nificent religious image rather than as a relic. Immediately after the first
exposition in 1357, Henri of Poitiers, Bishop of Troyes, is said to have forbid-
den further exhibitions, and when, in 1389, the de Charnys obtained papal
permission to show the Shroud again, another bishop of Troyes, Pierre d'Arcis,
twice wrote to Clement VII to protest. His principal objection, d'Arcis said,

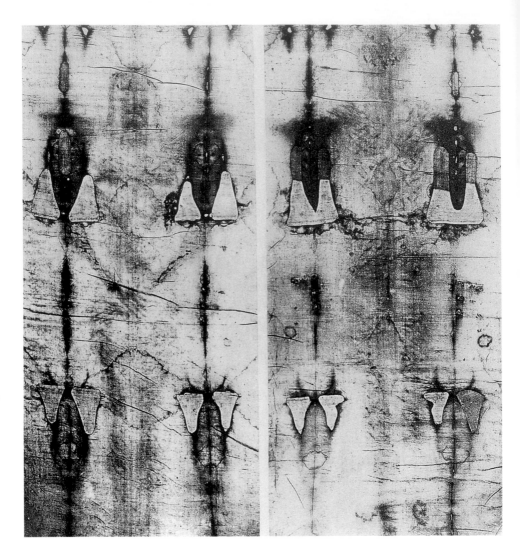

*T*he image branded as a
forgery by Pierre d'Arcis
(S. Pia, 1898: positive image).

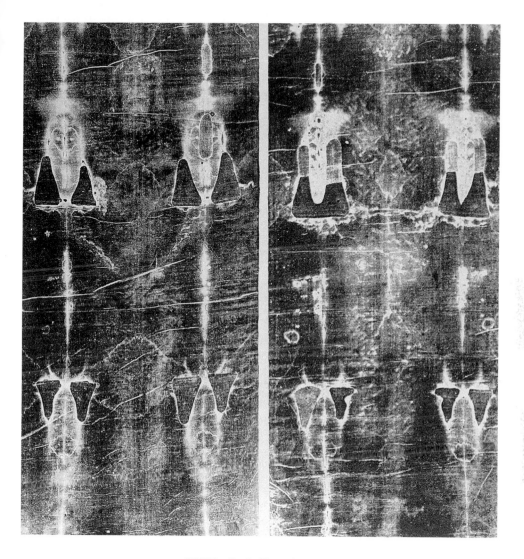

*T*he Turin Shroud remains
as controversial today as
it has been since Secondo Pia
first saw it in negative in 1898.

was based on a memorandum of
Henri of Poitiers, revealing that the
Lirey clergy had, 'falsely and deceit-
fully', obtained 'a certain cloth,
cunningly painted, upon which by a
clever sleight of hand was depicted
the twofold image of one man . . .
pretending that this was the actual
shroud in which our Saviour Jesus
Christ was enfolded' – a fact
'attested by the artist who had
painted it'.

This damning evidence has been
freely used by opponents of the
Shroud, seeking to brand it a
forgery. In the Middle Ages the
forging of religious relics was not
unknown; research has shown that
some 35 shrouds of Christ were
claimed in various places, at various
times. Some were plain lengths of
linen; others, such as the Shroud of
Besançon, bore images not dissimi-
lar to that on the Turin Shroud.

Most of these, however, including the Besançon example, can be shown to be
painted copies of the Turin cloth.

Against this evidence it may be noted that although the actual autograph of
d'Arcis's letter has survived, the claimed memorandum of Henri of Poitiers
has not, and might well itself have been a forgery by a powerful ecclesiastic

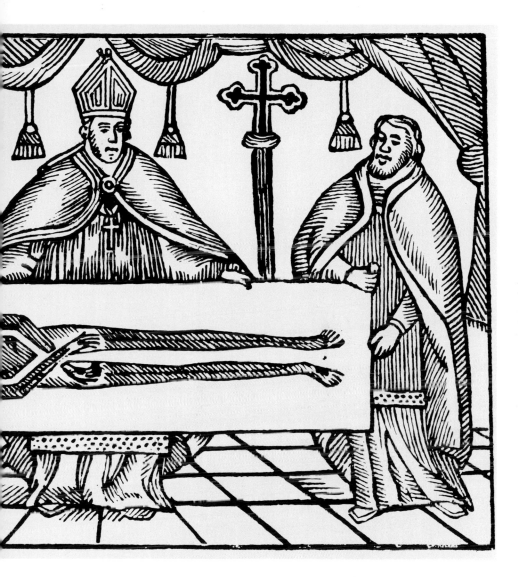

The exposition of the Holy Shroud of Besançon (17th-century devotional print).

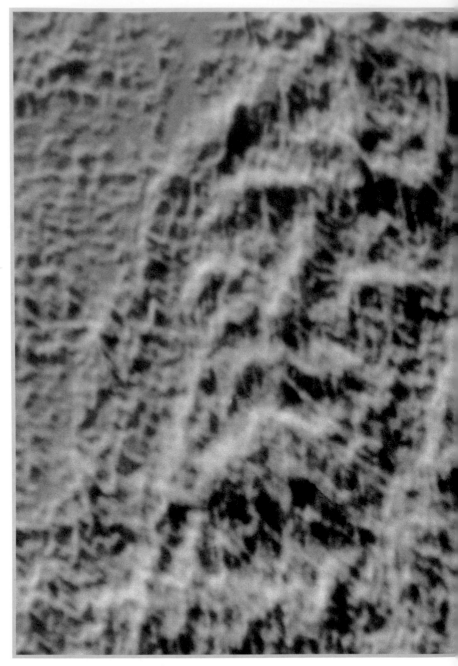

resentful of someone going over his head to petition papal permission for the expositions. Although much has been made of Clement's blood-relationship with the de Charnys, it seems unlikely that the pope would have been able to suppress d'Arcis's opposition so thoroughly had the memorandum been genuine. Had it existed, others would have seen it. Similarly, it is possible that the numerous copies of Besançon and elsewhere argue for the primacy – if not the authenticity – of the Turin Shroud.

Last is the argument from art. The Shroud is documented since 1357, yet no truly comparable medieval images exist. No one has yet explained satisfactorily how anyone, let alone a medieval forger, could have programmed so many hidden data into the relic; nor have they satisfactorily suggested why, even if they could, anyone should have encoded information which no one would be able to access for more than five centuries.

Though brushed aside by Clement VII, Bishop d'Arcis's claim has in recent years been taken as fact by those wishing to set aside the findings of STURP and other pro-Shroud researchers. For some years, the memorandum's most persistent advocate has been US microbiologist Walter McCrone, who had earlier exposed the so-called Vinland Map as a modern forgery. Never having seen the Shroud for himself, McCrone was given access to debris collected from the Shroud surface by the STURP team, which he quickly pronounced to be the remains of medieval artists' pigments. STURP's own findings were that the image was naturally formed, and that the pigmentation found scattered over the Shroud's surface was incidental, and not directly related to the image. Without in any way doubting Dr McCrone's professionalism,

The Shroud image yields up another secret to modern science: 3-D information is encoded in the negative image.

cause for concern for his objectivity might be found in a revealing statement made by him to an American journalist in 1980: 'The Shroud is a

27

fake, but I cannot prove it'. As with other contemporary detractors, one has the impression that McCrone had long ago made up his mind that the Shroud was a 'fake', and sought evidence to buttress his belief, rather than assessing the actual evidence.

The Evidence of Carbon-dating

At this period opinion hardened on both sides. Demands were increasingly heard for the cloth to undergo what was seen by many as the ultimate and definitive test, the dating of the cloth by measuring its carbon-14 content. Tiny amounts of the radioactive isotope carbon-14 are absorbed by all living things, and over time this decays at a fixed rate; calculating the rate of decay of the carbon-14 in an object theoretically permits the approximate time in history in which the object was alive to be fixed. Popularly, the accuracy of radiocarbon dating was held to be more or less absolute, and supporters and detractors of the Shroud alike believed that the test would settle the argument once and for all.

The Church finally agreed to the test. In April 1988 tiny samples of the cloth were taken, and forwarded to laboratories in Tucson, Arizona, in Oxford, and in Zurich, in Switzerland. With the Shroud samples went fragments of other ancient fabrics, whose ages were already known, to act as controls. The tests were co-ordinated by Dr Michael Tite of the British Museum. By the autumn all three laboratories had completed their work, and on 14 October the result was announced simultaneously in Turin, by Cardinal Ballestero, for the Church, and in London, by Dr Tite, for the three laboratories. The flax from which the linen of the Shroud had been woven had been harvested some time between 1260 and 1390. Around the world, the Turin Shroud was denounced as a 'forgery' by the media.

Stainless steel phials and silver-foil packet containing a sample of the Shroud for radiocarbon dating at the University of Oxford.

RELIGION

The Ever-Mysterious Sh

Even carbon dating may not confirm its

The three laboratories, one in Zurich, one in Oxford and one in Tucson, Ariz., have already delivered their findings to the British Museum. As soon as the results have been correlated, they are to be relayed to Turin, Italy, where the archbishop will prepare a formal statement. The report will provide the most definitive answer yet to the riddle of Christianity's best-known relic: is the Shroud of Turin old

coordinator, knew which

No matter what the arch cludes, the battle over the shro ticity will surely go on. If the show that the linen was in fact millennia ago, skeptics can dem that it actually wrapped the body of If the tests date the cloth to the M Ages, believers already have evide the fallibility of the carbon 14 proces

ert Hedges loads the sample wheel on to the ion source.

se to dating the
hroud of Turin

"If it is about 2,000 years old, ther impressed."

an obvious fake

Scientists beg
test on Turin

By ROB
SCIENT
gun tests
versity have be
Shroud, w
in which
fixion.
Profess
team at the
for Arch

a disc containing a s

lion i
ticles fr
radioac
the age

01

bs attacked aft

in Shroud
ts disput

rmed a

03

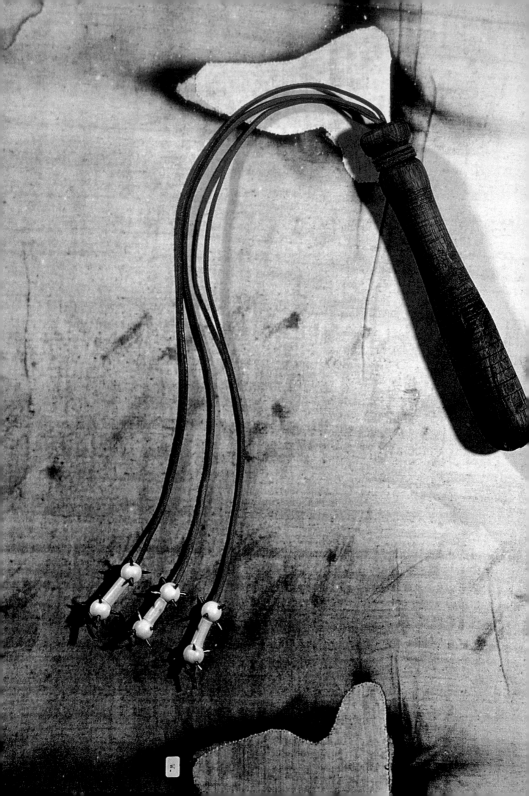

__R__econstruction of the scourge used on the man of the Shroud.

__M__onsignor Giulio Ricci, Vatican scholar, points out scourge-marks on a reproduction of the Shroud.

Almost immediately these tests, which should have settled the matter, themselves became a matter of controversy. The results had been leaked weeks before 14 October and persons not authorized to participate at the testings had been admitted: in both instances breaking the protocol agreed to beforehand. Far from it having been a blind testing, Dr Paul Damon of Tucson admitted that the distinctive weave of the Shroud had made it easy to recognize. For many, the most disturbing aspect of the whole thing was perhaps the glee with which certain scientists publicly exulted over the downfall of the Shroud. As Professor Hall of the Oxford laboratory told the press on 14 October, 'There was a multi-million-pound business in making forgeries during the fourteenth century. Someone just got a bit of linen, faked it up, and flogged it'. No mention of the unique and inexplicable nature of the image, which has never been reproduced satisfactorily. If nothing else, this contemptuous, and contemptible, statement demonstrates how thoroughly certain upholders of a rigid scientific orthodoxy had been rattled by the mystery of the Shroud.

In fact, it rapidly became clear that, apart from the scientists directly involved, almost no one was satisfied with the tests. Many believers found that the results did not disturb their belief, and said so; others felt that the tests themselves were faulty or improperly conducted (though there is no evidence to substantiate this), and wanted a re-testing – especially after it became widely known that all the radiocarbon dates published with the authority of the British Museum between 1980 and 1984 had been incorrect.

A mystery unresolved

Far from disappearing instantly from view, as its opponents had hoped, its mystery neatly eliminated by science, the Shroud continues to intrigue and baffle, and new studies continue to appear regularly. The evident failure of the scientific community to provide a sustainable explanation has meant that much of this new work is speculative and often simply bizarre. The German writers Holger Kersten and Elmar Gruber, for example, have tried to prove that the carbon-14 tests were 'fixed' by the Vatican, anxious to discredit the relic, but as the rest of their book is an attempt to show that Jesus survived the crucifixion

The face of Jesus as known to Christians worldwide (19th-century devotional impression of Veronica's Veil).

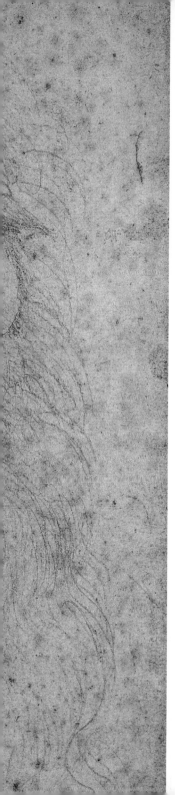

and moved to India, and as, for evidence of this, they need the Shroud to be genuine, their conspiracy-theory plea is easily understandable – while their evidence for this is not. Even weirder is the recent claim by Lynn Picknett and Clive Prince that the Shroud was forged by Leonardo da Vinci, who, having invented photography and joined the Priory of Sion, placed his own face on the cloth deliberately to subvert Christianity when eventually the truth was discovered in the future, as Leonardo foresaw it would be. This theory, ignoring equally the carbon-dating to well before da Vinci's birth and the image already witnessed to by d'Arcis in 1389, has been aptly compared by the writer Stuart Gordon not only to flogging a dead horse, but attempting to ride it at the same time.

Fortunately other researchers have a clearer grasp of the plausible, and the most rewarding research at present concerns itself with the actual nature of the image on the cloth. Although numbers of researchers are prepared to accept the carbon-14 dating, and are attempting to demonstrate how it was made in the 14th century, others again see the image as containing its own proof of authenticity. Even

*I*t has recently been suggested,
somewhat unconvincingly, that
Leonardo da Vinci forged the Shroud.

*T*he Resurrection,
   by the
15th-century artist,
Raffaellino del Garbo.

at the time when the test results were being leaked in 1988, the English expert on medieval painting Anna Hulbert said that the idea that the Shroud could be dated only from the 14th century raised 'more problems [for] an art historian than if it [was] genuinely the Shroud of Jesus'. If one accepts that, for whatever reason, the radiocarbon dating was suspect and that substantial support for the Shroud's genuineness is derived from all the other evidence, then the words of the archaeologist Dr Eugenia Nitowski to Ian Wilson should be considered:

> In any form of enquiry or scientific discipline, it is the weight of evidence which must be considered conclusive. In archaeology, if there are ten lines of evidence, carbon dating being one of them, and it conflicts with the other nine, there is little hesitation to throw out the carbon date as inaccurate.

Which leaves us – with what? With a deepening mystery. Far from being solved, for most open-minded people, the jury is still out on the Holy Shroud of Turin, and is likely to remain so for some considerable time to come.

*T**he Man in the
Shroud – the
real face of Jesus?***

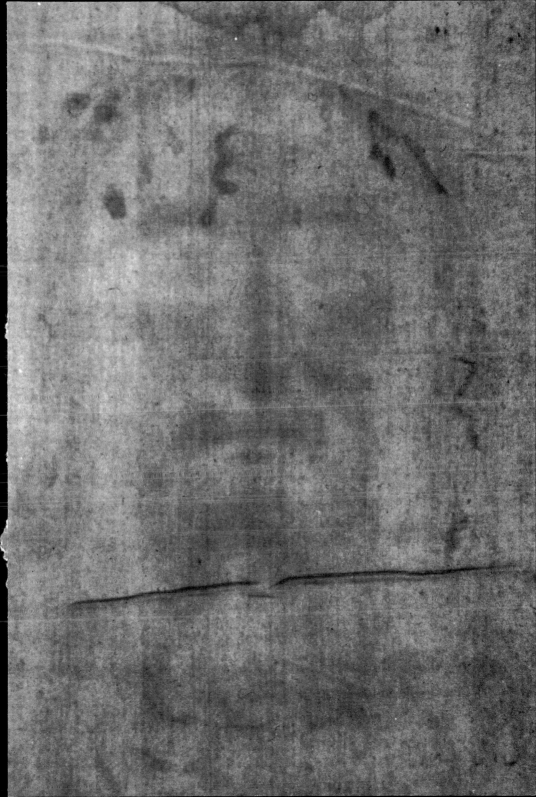

THE HOLY
SHROUD

PHOTOGRAPHIC ACKNOWLEDGEMENTS
Cover AKG London; page 3 SCALA/Galleria
Sabauda, Torino; p. 4 AKG; pp. 6, 7 Fortean
Picture Library [FPL]/ Tristan Gray Hulse
[TGH]; pp. 8–9, 10 AKG; pp. 11, 12–13 SCALA;
p. 15 FPL/TGH; p. 16 FPL; p. 18 FPL/TGH;
p. 10 FPL; p. 21 e.t. archive; pp. 22, 23, 24–5
FPL/TGH; p. 26 AKG; p. 29 Science Photo
Library; pp. 30, 31 Ancient Art & Architecture;
p. 33 FPL/TGH; pp. 34–5 SCALA/ Biblioteca
Reale, Torino; pp. 36–7 SCALA/ Accadmia,
Firenze; p. 39 AKG.

First published in Great Britain 1997
by George Weidenfeld and Nicolson Ltd
The Orion Publishing Group
5 Upper St Martin's Lane
London WC2H 9EA

A CIP catalogue record for this book is available
from the British Library
ISBN 0 297 823019

Picture Research: Suzanne Williams

Designed by Harry Green

Typeset in Baskerville